WINNING OVER SUICIDE

Understanding and Overcoming Suicidal and Depressive thoughts.

TABLE OF CONTENT

Chapter 1

Introduction

Depression and depressive diseases are categorized as mood disorders in the medical sector, spanning anything from Major Depression to Dysthymia. They have a lot of symptoms that influence individuals socially, occupationally, educationally, interpersonally, etc. How can one get depressed? Here's how it works: the nerves in our brain don't contact each other, but rather convey signals from one to the next via chemicals called neurotransmitters. We need precisely the appropriate quantity of this substance between the nerves to give identical information to the next nerve. If there isn't enough of that chemical, the message doesn't get sent through appropriately and in this situation, depression or a depressive disease might ensue. When it comes to depression illnesses the chemicals most usually out of balance are serotonin and norepinephrine. A person struggling with depression frequently feels radically different thinking before and after a depressing episode. This might be a consequence of a chemical imbalance and can lead to the individual not knowing the solutions available to assist them to ease their misery. Many individuals who suffer from depression describe feeling as if they've lost the capacity to anticipate a joyful future or recall a happy past. Often people don't understand they're suffering from a curable condition, and seeking treatment may not even cross their thoughts. Emotions and even physical pain may become overwhelming. They don't want to die, but it's the only way they believe their misery will cease. It is a completely illogical decision. Suffering from depression is involuntary, much like cancer or diabetes, but it is a curable condition that can be handled.

Everyone feels depressed at times. The termination of a relationship or a poor grade might contribute to low mood. Sometimes melancholy comes on for no apparent cause. Depression, contra regular sadness, is defined by longer and deeper emotions of melancholy and the presence of specific diagnostic symptoms. This difference is significant, since, in extreme situations, depression may be life-threatening, with suicide as a potential conclusion. Depressed individuals may also fail to live up to their potential, performing badly in school and lingering on the social edges. Depression is widely overlooked or mistreated; the disease often hinders individuals from taking action to improve themselves.

Signs of Depression

Anyone who feels low most of the day virtually every day for weeks or months may be clinically depressed. Depressed persons may experience:

Loss of enjoyment in nearly all activities
Feelings of tiredness or lack of energy
Frequent tearfulness
Difficulty with concentration or memory
A disruption in sleep pattern, with either too much or too little sleep; the individual may wake up in the night or early morning and not feel refreshed the following day
An increase or reduction in appetite, with a corresponding change in weight
Markedly reduced interest in sex
Sentiments of worthlessness and self-blame or excessive feelings of remorse
Unrealistic beliefs and anxieties (e.g., thinking no one like them or that they have a fatal disease when there is no supporting evidence) (e.g., believing no one like them or that they have a terminal illness when there is no supporting proof)
Hopelessness regarding the future and thoughts of suicide

What Causes Depression?

There is emerging evidence that depression is in part a disorder with a biological foundation. It is more frequent in those with close relatives who have been depressed. Research on the physiology of the nervous system reveals that the degree of activity of neurotransmitters, such as norepinephrine and serotonin, alters in persistent depression: Antidepressant drugs presumably function by correcting a "chemical imbalance" of this type. One sort of imbalance is connected with bipolar illness (originally termed manic depression), marked by severe mood swings from sadness to anger or exhilaration and other symptoms. A variety of medical diseases may also contribute to depression: An evaluation by a medical physician may be beneficial to rule out medical reasons for depression symptoms.

While depression does seem to have biological components, it is apparent that psychological and social variables also play a key role. The death of a loved one or a disappointment may precipitate depression; prior losses, sometimes not completely addressed, can make someone more sensitive to sadness. For complicated causes, some persons find themselves immersed in negative modes of thinking, which may lead to depression. Other environmental components include a lack of social support and the unavailability of options for satisfaction.

Suicide

Suicide is the second biggest cause of death among young people. A significant cause of suicide is a mental disease, particularly typically depression. People feeling suicidal are overwhelmed by painful emotions and see death as the only way out, losing sight of the fact that suicide is a permanent "solution" to a temporary state—most people who try to kill themselves but live later say they are glad they didn't die. Most people who die by suicide could have been helped. A person contemplating suicide often confides in a friend, who may be able to encourage them to seek help. When the danger is considerable, concerned friends and family should seek expert counsel. Suicidal thoughts may be transitory or more frequent, passive (e.g., "What if I were dead?"), or active (e.g., thinking of methods to kill oneself, planning a plan) (e.g., thinking of ways to kill oneself, making a plan). Preparations for death, such as giving up goods or getting a gun, are the reason for significant fear. A sudden boost in spirits in a depressed individual might be a warning indication that they are about to murder themselves. Any amount of suicidal thoughts should be treated seriously.

How Can You Tell if Suicide Is a Possibility?

While suicide is generally impossible to anticipate, there are several warning signs:

Being depressed or having other mental problems
Talking directly or indirectly about wanting to die or "not be around"
Increased social isolation
Significant changes in appearance and hygiene
Giving away valuable belongings; making other preparations for death
A quick shift in mood
While anybody may become suicidal, several risk factors make suicide more likely:

Previous suicide attempt(s) (s)
Having a family member or acquaintance who just murdered themself; many suicides in the community
Other recent, important losses, such as the loss of a relationship or career
Cultural and religious views promoting suicide (e.g., notion that suicide is a noble

resolve of a personal crisis) (e.g., belief that suicide is a noble resolution of a personal dilemma)

Alcohol and drug misuse (since this might weaken inhibitions and promote impulsiveness) (as this can lower inhibitions and increase impulsiveness)

Feelings of despair

Access to means of suicide (e.g., a pistol, several pills) (e.g., a gun, some pills)

Unwillingness to seek assistance and hurdles to receiving mental health treatment

Misconceptions About Suicide

"People who speak about it won't do it."

Suicide threats should always be taken seriously. The fact is that few folks are single-minded in their resolve to kill themselves; many are seeking aid even while they consider suicide.

"People who wish to harm themselves are beyond help."

Fortunately, this is not the case. Suicidal urges may be powerful yet short-lived. The majority of persons who are suicidal even for lengthy periods recover and may benefit from therapy.

"Suicide is an entirely personal choice."

This argument is occasionally used to defend a "hands-off" approach. It is a myth since suicide doesn't simply affect the individual who dies; it affects others too.
"Asking about suicide might put the thought in someone's head."

Research indicates that asking someone about suicide would not "place the notion in their brain." Many persons with suicidal thoughts frequently feel relief when someone asks. Suicidal persons are involved in a secret fight with thoughts of death. Talking about the prospect of suicide might relieve the loneliness of the battle and can be a first step toward receiving treatment.

How Can I Help a Depressed Person?

It helps to listen in a way that shows you care and empathize. This does not imply joining in the person's sorrow; an attitude of guarded optimism is required. However, avoid diminishing the person's distress or making statements like "Everything's OK" or "Your life is good—you do not need to be suicidal!" Try saying something like "I can understand how hopeless you feel, but I think things can get better" or "I hear you; I want to help." Advise should be basic and practical; for example, "Let's go on a stroll and chat more" or "I am here for you, but you need more expert advice; let's check up some figures together."

Change may be gradual. Trying to assist someone who is sad and is not responding to your efforts may be difficult and anxiety-producing. It's crucial to take care of yourself and obtain assistance, too. If you don't take care of yourself, you may burn out, feel angry, or give up on the person. It is a good idea to seek help and support well before you reach this point.

If a person is expressing that they have suicidal thoughts or you see signs of possible suicidality, it's important to take it seriously. Sometimes, a suicidal individual may want you to keep your predicament a secret. It might be tempting to pledge to keep this secret and/or to take on the responsibility of supporting them all on your own; nevertheless, these are not smart ideas. Consider the probable implications of neglecting to seek individual professional assistance. It is a show of care to obtain treatment for someone who is in danger of killing themselves, even if it makes them furious with you.

The diagnosis and treatment of depression and depressive diseases may be done by a medical doctor, or mental health experts such as a psychologist, social worker, or psychotherapist. However, if we notice and pay attention to the signs of depression, we may assist these experts in better treating the disorder.

Please note: Other conditions and some drugs may create symptoms that mirror the signs of sadness. A complete medical examination should be performed to rule out the presence of other medical conditions potentially causing depressive symptoms. It's normal to feel some of the following symptoms from time to time, but experiencing several or more for more than two or three weeks may indicate the presence of depression or another depressive illness. Remember, you must seek a professional for an accurate diagnosis of depression.

Depression in Youth
Many suicidal children and adolescents have clinical depression alone or in connection with another mental diseases such as anxiety disorder, attention deficit disorder, bipolar illness (manic depression), or child-onset schizophrenia. Each child's personality, biological composition, and surroundings are unique, and depression and suicide thoughts in children are complicated concerns involving many aspects. By detecting and treating children we may enhance the possibility a young person with depression can have a longer, healthier, more quality life.

In addition to the normal symptoms of sadness, and warning signs of suicide watch for the following in children:

Verbal cues
Behavioral clues\sHigh risk children
An attempt or suicidal activity.

Know What To Do

Because children aren't always able to grasp and articulate their emotions, as adults we must be more diligent in identifying the ways depression and suicide appear in children, and seek to get them the care they need.

It is a fallacy that depression is part of the aging process. It is not typical for individuals of any age to suffer from depression; this includes our old population. Major depression (sometimes known as clinical depression) is a medical disease. It is a chemical imbalance in the brain and may emerge in anybody regardless of age, ethnicity, or economic background. The sickness might occur after a triggering event or for no apparent cause at all.

Chapter 2

Suicide and suicidal behavior

Suicide is the act of taking one's own life on purpose. Suicidal conduct is any activity that might lead a person to die, such as taking a drug overdose or wrecking a vehicle on purpose.

Causes

Suicide and suicidal tendencies generally occur in persons with one or more of the following:

Bipolar disorder
Borderline personality disorder
Depression
Drug or alcohol usage
Post-traumatic stress disorder (PTSD)
Schizophrenia
History of physical, sexual, or emotional abuse

Stressful life circumstances, such as major financial or marital problems
People who attempt to take their own life are typically seeking to get away from a circumstance that appears difficult to cope with. Many who attempt suicide are seeking solace from:

Feeling humiliated, guilty, or like a burden to others
Feeling like a victim
Feelings of rejection, loss, or loneliness
Suicidal behaviors may arise when there is a circumstance or event that the individual finds overwhelming, such as:

Aging (older persons have the greatest risk of suicide) (older people have the highest rate of suicide)
Death of a loved one
Drug or alcohol usage
Emotional trauma
Serious physical sickness or suffering
Unemployment or money troubles

Risk factors for suicide among youth include:

Access to firearms
A family member who committed suicide
History of injuring oneself on purpose
History of being ignored or mistreated
Living in places where there have been recent epidemics of suicide among young people
Romantic breakup
While males are more likely than women to die by suicide, women are twice as likely to attempt suicide.

Most suicide attempts do not end in death. Many of these efforts are done in a manner that makes rescue feasible. These efforts are typically a cry for assistance.
Some individuals try suicide in a method that is less likely to be lethal, such as poisoning or overdose. Men are more likely to use violent means, such as shooting themselves. As a consequence, suicide

attempts by males are more likely to end in death.
Relatives of persons who try or accomplish suicide may blame themselves or get extremely furious. They may regard the suicide attempt as selfish. However, persons who attempt suicide frequently incorrectly assume that they are doing their friends and families a service by taking themselves out of the world.

Any mental health problem that may have led to the suicide attempt should be investigated and addressed. This includes:

Bipolar disorder
Borderline personality disorder
Drug or alcohol dependency
Major depression
Schizophrenia
Post-traumatic stress disorder (PTSD)
Always take suicide attempts and threats seriously.

When to Contact a Medical Professional
Contact a health care practitioner immediately away if you or someone you know is experiencing thoughts of suicide. The client requires mental health treatment straight now. DO NOT disregard the individual as merely attempting to seek attention. I

Why Do Teens Try to Kill Themselves?
Most youths questioned after making a suicide attempt report that they did it because they were attempting to escape from a situation that appeared tough to cope with or to find relief from particularly awful thoughts or sensations. They didn't want to die as much as they wanted to flee from what was going on. And at that specific time death looked like the only way out.

Some persons who end their lives or attempt suicide can be seeking to escape emotions of rejection, pain, or loss. Others could feel furious, humiliated, or guilty over something. Some individuals may be apprehensive about disappointing friends or family members. And others may feel unwanted, unloved, mistreated, or that they're a burden to others.

We all feel overwhelmed by harsh feelings or events occasionally. But most individuals get through it or can put their issues in perspective and find a way to move on with tenacity and optimism. So why does one individual attempt suicide whereas another person in the same stressful scenario does not? What makes some individuals more resilient (better able to cope with life's setbacks and problems) than others? What makes a person unable to see any way out of a horrible position than taking their life? The answer to such questions resides in the fact that most persons who die by suicide suffer depression.

Depression drives individuals to concentrate largely on failures and disappointments, to stress the bad aspect of their conditions, and to underestimate their qualities or value. Someone with severe depression can't see the prospect of a positive end and may feel they will never be happy or things will never go well for them again.

Depression influences a person's ideas in such a manner that the individual doesn't understand when an issue may be overcome. It's as if the sadness puts a filter on the person's thoughts that distorts things. That's why sad individuals don't comprehend that suicide is a permanent solution to a transitory issue in the same way that other people do. A youngster with depression may feel that there's no other way out of trouble, no other escape from mental agony, or no other method to voice a desperate discontent.

Sometimes individuals who feel suicidal may not even recognize they are sad. They're oblivious that it is the depression — not the issue — that's pushing them to view things in a "there's no way out," "it will never get better," and "there's nothing I can do" type of attitude.

When depression lifts because someone obtains the correct therapy or treatment, the skewed thinking is cleansed. The individual may rediscover joy, vitality, and hope again. But when someone is genuinely sad, suicidal thought is a significant risk.

People with a disease called bipolar disorder are also more at risk for suicide since their illness may lead them to go through moments when they are exceedingly sad as well as times when they have unusually high or frenzied energy (called mania or manic) (called mania or manic). Both of these severe periods of bipolar disease influence and distort a person's mood, viewpoint, and judgment. For those with this disease, it might be difficult to keep situations in perspective and behave with sound judgment.

Substance Abuse

Teens with alcohol and drug issues are also more at risk for suicide ideation and conduct. Alcohol and certain medications have depressing effects on the brain. Misuse of these drugs may bring on significant depression. That's especially true for some teens who already tend towards depression because of their biology, family history, or other life stressors.

The problem can be made worse because many people who are depressed turn to alcohol or drugs as an escape. But they may not realize that the depressive effects alcohol and drugs have on the brain can intensify depression in the long run. Besides their negative effects, alcohol and narcotics alter a person's judgment. They interfere with the capacity to evaluate danger, make smart decisions, and conceive solutions to issues. Many suicide attempts occur while someone is under the influence of alcohol or drugs.

This doesn't imply that everyone who is sad or who has an alcohol or drug problem will attempt to kill themselves, of course. But both diseases – particularly when combined – enhance a person's risk for suicide.

Suicide Is Not Always Planned
Sometimes a sad individual prepares a suicide in advance. Many times, however, suicide attempts come spontaneously, at a moment of feeling profoundly distraught. A circumstance like a divorce, a large battle with a parent, an unwanted pregnancy, being outed by someone else, or being victimized in any manner might lead someone to feel passionately distressed. Often, a situation like this, on top of an existing depression, acts like the final straw.

Other individuals who attempt suicide intend to die and some aren't convinced they want to die. For others, a suicide attempt is a means to vent severe emotional sorrow. They can't explain how they feel, thus, for them, trying suicide seems like the only way to get their message out. Sadly, many individuals who truly didn't plan to kill themselves find up dead or very sick.

What Are the Warning Signs of Suicide?
Often, there are clues that someone may be thinking about or preparing for a suicide attempt. Here are some of them:

talking about suicide or death in general
talking about "going away" referring to stuff they "won't be needing," and giving away assets
talking about feeling hopeless or feeling guilty pulling away from friends or family and losing the urge to go out having no want to take part in favorite tasks or activities trouble focusing or thinking clearly changes in eating or sleeping routines
self-destructive behaviors (drinking alcohol, doing drugs, or cutting, for example)

(drinking alcohol, taking drugs, or cutting, for example)

How Can I Cope With Problems?

Being a teen is not easy. There are many new social, academic, and personal pressures. And for people who have other problems to deal with, such as living in violent or abusive environments, life can feel even harder.

Some teens worry about sexuality and relationships, wondering if their feelings and attractions are normal, or if they will be loved and accepted. Others battle with body image and eating disorders – attempting to meet an unrealistic ideal leaves them feeling horrible about themselves.

Some teenagers have learning challenges or attention problems that make it challenging for them to excel in school. They may feel dissatisfied with themselves or believe they are a disappointment to others.

These difficulties may be stressful and taxing — and can lead to depression if they carry on too long without respite or help. We all struggle with painful problems and events at times. How do people get through it without becoming depressed? Part of it is staying connected to family, friends, school, faith, and other support networks.

People are better able to cope when they have at least one person who believes in them, wants the best for them, and in whom they can confide. It also helps to keep in mind that most problems are temporary and can be overcome.

When struggling with problems, try to:

Tell someone you trust what's going on with you.
Be with folks who are compassionate and positive.

Ask someone to assist you to figure out what to do about a situation you're encountering. Work with a therapist or counselor if things are making you down and depressed — or if you don't have a solid support network or believe you can't deal.

Counselors and therapists may give emotional support and can help teenagers establish their coping strategies for dealing with challenges. It might also help to join a support network for others who are going through the same challenges — for example, anorexia and body image issues, coping with an alcoholic family member, or sexuality and sexual health concerns. These groups may assist create a loving atmosphere where you can speak about difficulties with individuals who share your worries.

How Can I Help a Friend?

It is always a good idea to start a discussion with someone you suspect may be contemplating suicide. It enables you to obtain assistance for the individual, and

simply talking about it may make the person feel less alone and more cared for and understood.
Talking things out also may offer the individual an opportunity to examine alternative solutions to challenges. Most of the time, individuals who are contemplating suicide are eager to chat if someone asks them out of concern and compassion. Because sad individuals are not as able to see solutions as well as others, it might assist to have someone work with them in coming up with at least one alternative way out of a difficult circumstance.

Even if a friend or classmate swears you to secrecy, you must get help as soon as possible — your friend's life could depend on it. Someone who is seriously thinking about suicide may have sunk so deeply into an emotional hole that they can't see that they need help. Tell an adult you trust as soon as possible.

Sometimes, youths who make a suicide attempt — or who die from suicide — appear to provide no sign beforehand. This might leave loved ones feeling not just sorrow-stricken but guilty and wondering whether they overlooked anything. Their family members and friends need to know that sometimes there is no warning and they should not blame themselves.

When someone dies by suicide, the people left behind can wrestle with terrible emotional pain. Teens who have experienced a recent loss or crisis or who had a family member or classmate who died by suicide may be at risk for suicidal ideation and conduct themselves.

If you've been close to someone who has tried or committed suicide, it might help to chat with a therapist or counselor – someone who is skilled in dealing with this complicated subject.

Chapter 3

The Psychology of Suicide

Those who have known someone who has taken their own life will constantly ask themselves this question: "Why? Why did they do it?" This question typically leads to a tornado of negative thought patterns, and occasionally individuals might even come to blame themselves. For this reason, it is necessary to comprehend the plain facts of suicide—a clinical viewpoint on the topic that may help us understand the psyche of someone who has pondered or tried suicide.

Various risk factors might lead to a suicide attempt. Some of the most typical ones include a history of depression, being in a difficult life circumstance, and having a disrupted family background. But suicide may emerge from unexpected sources as well—for instance, a recognized adverse effect for many drugs that treat mental health issues is a beginning or escalation of suicidal thoughts or behaviors. There are so many elements that might play into suicidal thoughts that it's crucial to keep an eye out for any indicator that you or someone you know, no matter how happy you or they may appear, may be in danger of wishing to inflict self-harm.

Suicide is one of the top causes of death in our nation. Many people assume that despair is the only reason for the choice to try suicide—however, this isn't accurate. For example, one study showed that although depression is seen in some individuals who are suicidal, only roughly 5% of persons who are depressed commit suicide. Genetic variables and stressful life conditions play a considerably greater impact than previously considered, leading me to feel that they should be among the first things taken into account when treating someone who is/was suicidal. If someone you know has recently been fired or come out of a terrible divorce or lost someone important to them, make care to check in periodically, even if they have never experienced depression prior.

I can tell you as someone with personal experience in this area that in my situation, the major reason motivating me to desire to kill myself is both the sensation of overwhelming terror and the worry of becoming a burden on others. If you are worried that your existence is pointless and that others would be better off without you—that's a major red flag. Sometimes, it might come down to indifference and exhaustion: some individuals feel so extremely bored out by their condition that they simply don't want to be alive anymore. Their area of vision becomes so limited that they either forget or don't care about individuals who they could impact. In all honesty, it might even look like a selfish inclination to the individuals in the lives of those who are suicidal. But one thing I can tell you is that suicide does not generally arise out of vengeance or resentment. People don't typically take their life to damage others—in fact, they misguidedly aim to accomplish the opposite.

If you or someone you know is in danger, be sure to get them to care quickly. Get them to a safe location if you can, and if you ever need to, do not feel afraid to call emergency services or hotlines. Even if someone you know constantly jokes about suicide, this might be a covert cry for assistance, so have an open talk if you can. Treat yourself and others carefully and with compassion, and make sure the people in your life know how much they matter to you. And remember, suicide is not the fault of the individual who commits it, nor is it the responsibility of the people around them. Blame will do nothing except exacerbate the agony.

The origins of suicidal conduct are not entirely known; yet, this activity certainly stems from the complex interplay of several elements. Although several risk factors have been identified, they typically do not explain why individuals attempt to end their life. In this Review, we summarize major recent findings in theoretical, clinical, and empirical psychology research concerning the formation of suicidal thoughts and behavior, and underline the essential relevance of psychological determinants. Personality and individual differences, cognitive variables, social features, and bad life experiences are major contributors to suicidal conduct. Most persons coping with suicidal thoughts and behavior do not obtain therapy. Some research shows that different kinds of cognitive and behavioral therapy may lessen the risk of suicide reattempt, but almost any information concerning variables that protect against suicide is available. The development of novel psychological and psychosocial therapies demands urgent attention. Introduction Suicide is the 14th biggest cause of death globally, accounting for 1·5% of total mortality. Although psychological factors such as risk-taking and decision-making can affect the risk of other causes of death (eg, heart disease and cancer), suicide is perhaps the cause of death most directly affected by psychological factors, because a person makes a conscious decision to end his or her own life. Therefore, knowledge of suicide and the development of strategies to anticipate and prevent its occurrence are the duty of psychologists, psychiatrists, and allied mental health specialists. Earlier papers have presented broad evaluations of the subject of suicide. In this Review, we analyze and synthesize current information regarding the psychology of suicidal conduct, including psychological theories of suicidal behavior, risk and protective variables, psychological therapies, and significant areas for psychological research into this important issue. The objective of this is to present an overview of some of the most fascinating and essential findings regarding the psychology of suicidal behavior.

Personality and individual differences, cognitive factors, social aspects, and negative life events are key contributors to suicidal behavior. Most persons coping with suicidal thoughts and behavior do not obtain therapy. Some evidence suggests that different forms of cognitive and behavioral therapies can reduce the risk of suicide reattempt, but hardly any evidence about factors that protect against suicide is available. The development of novel psychological and psychosocial therapies demands urgent attention.
Suicide is the 14th biggest cause of death globally, accounting for 1·5% of total mortality. Although psychological factors such as risk-taking and decision-making can affect the risk of other causes of death (eg,

heart disease and cancer), suicide is perhaps the cause of death most directly affected by psychological factors, because a person makes a conscious decision to end his or her own life. Therefore, understanding suicide and developing methods to predict and prevent its occurrence is the responsibility of psychologists, psychiatrists, and related mental health professionals.

Psychological research is ideally situated to increase the knowledge of why some individuals attempt suicide while others do not. Understanding the psychological processes that underpin both suicidal ideation and the decision to act on suicidal thoughts is particularly important because interventions should be targeted at addressing suicidal ideation when it fi first emerges before it progresses to a suicide attempt.

Suicidal desire is a necessary though not sufficient cause for a suicide attempt.

However, if a person with high suicidal desire acquires the capability to attempt suicide, then the risk of a serious suicide attempt is increased. Acquired capability comprises reduced fear of death and increased tolerance for physical pain. According to the theory, exposure to and encounters with previous painful experiences increase an individual's tolerance for the physical-pain aspects of self-harm through habituation processes. The core components of the theory have attracted considerable research attention. Second, the integrated motivational-volitional model of suicidal conduct conceptualizes suicide as a behavior (rather than a result of mental diseases) that evolves via motivational and volitional stages The motivational phase discusses the elements that drive the development of suicidal ideas and intent, while the volitional phase defines the factors that decide whether a person commits suicide. This model merges the major variables from preceding ideas into a thorough map of the suicidal process from thoughts to actions of suicide. Whereas belongingness and burdensomeness are paramount in the final common pathway to suicide in the interpersonal theory, feelings of defeat (ie, feeling defeated after triggering circumstances) and entrapment (ie, unable to escape from stressful, humiliating, or defeating circumstances) are posited to be of most importance within the integrated motivational-volitional model. When an individual feels both defeated and trapped, the likelihood that suicidal ideation will emerge increases when motivational moderators (eg, low levels of social support) are present. The interpersonal theory of suicide posits that acquired capability establishes behavioral enaction (ie, suicide attempts), it is just one of several (volitional phase) factors within the integrated motivational-volitional model posited to increase the likelihood of a suicide attempt. Such factors include exposure to the suicidal behavior of others, impulsivity, and having access to the means of suicide. Although the integrated motivational-volitional paradigm is new, empirical data supports its effectiveness.

Psychological risk and protective factors: The variables related to suicide risk may be classified into four groups: personality and individual differences, cognitive issues, social factors, and unpleasant life experiences. In reviewing these factors, I summarised what is known to date, but do not exhaustively describe the potential mechanisms through which these factors might affect suicidal behavior, which is an extremely important goal for future research. I selected these factors because they feature in the theoretical models, have received research attention in the literature, or are promising candidates for the future. Each of these factors might contribute to the emergence of suicide risk independently or together with other factors. Some of the factors are associated with the emergence of suicidal ideation, whereas others increase the likelihood that suicidal thoughts will be acted on.

Personality and individual differences: Factors related to personality and individual differences are of interest because they are fairly stable in adulthood, often have known biological bases, are affected by the environment, and affect cognition and emotion.

Hopelessness scores in a 10-year prospective study of patients admitted to hospital with suicidal ideation. However, findings from a 12-year perspective showed that when suicidal intent was compared with hopelessness, hopelessness was a non-significant predictor of suicide. More recently, in a small study of people who attempted suicide, hopelessness did not significantly predict future suicide attempts in a 4-year follow-up when past suicide-attempt history and entrapment were included in the analysis. These more recent mixed findings suggest that although hopelessness is important in the development of suicidal ideation (consistent with theoretical models), other factors might be more useful in the prediction of actual suicide attempts or deaths.

Perfectionism: Growing evidence suggests that perfectionism is associated with suicidal ideation and suicide attempts, although few prospective clinical studies have been done. Perfectionism can be defined in different ways and not all types are equally associated with suicide risk. One type, socially prescribed perfectionism (defined as the belief that other people [eg, family members] hold unrealistically high expectations of you), is most consistently associated with suicidal thoughts and attempts, especially when these socially determined beliefs are internalized as self-criticism. Recent research suggests that the social dimensions of perfectionism increase suicide risk by promoting a sense of social disconnection, which is consistent with the integrated motivational-volitional model and interpersonal theory of suicide. In particular, perfectionistic beliefs can also interact with other factors (eg, negative life events, adversity, and cognitions) to impede recovery from a suicidal episode or increase the risk of suicidal ideation and self-harm further.

The big five personality dimensions are neuroticism, extroversion, agreeableness, openness to experience, and conscientiousness. In basic terms, high levels of neuroticism and low levels of extroversion are connected with suicidal thoughts, attempts, and completions. The combined effects of high neuroticism and low extroversion might be stronger predictors of suicide than neuroticism alone. The proposed interaction is consistent with predominant theories, suggesting that people of such have an increased risk of suicide.

Low levels of optimism are connected with self-harm in teenage females. Optimism has also been demonstrated to buffer the relationship between despair and suicide thoughts.

Cognitive rigidity For decades, clinical and theoretical perspectives have depicted suicidal patients as being cognitively inflexible or inflexible, leading to the conclusion that suicide is the only alternative. Findings from trials in which behavioral measures of cognitive rigidity are delivered to suicide attempters and clinical controls have offered credence to this view.

Rumination, which refers to persistent concentration on an individual's sensations of misery, has been related to suicide ideas and attempts. A distinction has been noted between brooding rumination, in which a person dwells on his or her symptoms, and reflective pondering, in which a person contemplates the reasons for his or her symptoms and potential solutions, with brooding rumination being more strongly associated with suicidal thoughts and attempts. Rumination has also been connected with higher feelings of despair, hopelessness, and worse problem-solving; an essential objective for future study is to establish how these characteristics can interact together to enhance the risk of suicide action.

Thought suppression refers to efforts to purposefully cease thinking of unpleasant ideas.

Personal goal pursuit defines identity, and how people adjust when a goal becomes unattainable is known to affect wellbeing. Indeed, evidence suggests that suicide attempters who tend not to re-engage with new goals (in the face of existing unattainable goals) are at increased risk of readmission to hospital after self-harm, with this association being further affected by the extent of existing goal disengagement. Reasons for a living have been studied extensively in the prediction of suicidal ideation and attempts, and have been incorporated into treatment protocols. Good evidence suggests that individuals with few reasons for living are at increased risk of suicidal thinking and attempts Related to reasons for living, in a 10-year follow-up study, psychiatric outpatients who had a moderate-to-strong desire to die and little desire to live were at increased risk of suicide. Defeat and entrapment Defeat and entrapment have received substantial attention within social-rank theories of depression, scientific literature about arrested flight, and most recently in the integrated motivational-volitional model. The inability to escape from defeating or stressful circumstances provides the setting conditions for the emergence of suicidal thoughts. Although defeat and entrapment are widely known ideas within the psychopathology literature, their use in suicide research off ers great potential. Indeed, both defeat and entrapment differentiate suicidal patients from controls irrespective of depression and despair, and both predict suicidal thoughts and attempts over time. Entrapment has also been proven to predict recurrent suicide attempts in 4 years beyond established risk indicators for suicide. Social considerations Suicide does not occur in a social vacuum. Family history of suicide increases the risk of suicide; this effect is independent of a family history of mental disease and is hence partially indicative of a social transmission effect. Exposure to suicide behaviors of relatives or friends is also connected with similar tendencies in teenagers. Maternal suicide behavior might be more strongly connected with off spring suicidal behaviour than paternal suicidal activity, and children are more likely to be affected by parental suicidal conduct than adolescents or adults. Although psychological causes (eg, modeling effects) require additional empirical research, portrayals of suicide in the media may affect rates of suicide. The effect of the internet on suicide conduct deserves additional investigation since it could have both negatives (eg, discouraging assistance seeking) and positive (eg, source of support or signposting) effects. Indeed, research findings indicated that approximately 20% of teenagers stated that the internet or social networking sites influenced their choice to self-harm. Psychological factors (including contagion, imitation, suggestion, identifi -cation, social learning, and assortative homophily or susceptibility) are also linked to the formation of suicide clusters. Social isolation and the lack of social support are proven correlates of suicide risk and are significant components in modern theories of suicidal conduct. Any evaluation of suicide risk should, as a matter of course, consider the degree to which a susceptible person is socially isolated.

Negative life occurrences Childhood adversities; Many studies have demonstrated a high link between the incidence of bad life experiences throughout childhood (eg, physical, sexual, and emotional abuse; family violence; and parental sickness, divorce, or death) and the eventual experience of suicidal conduct. These research findings demonstrated a high dose–response connection between the number of kinds of adversities and the future likelihood of suicide attempts. Sexual and physical abuse during childhood are especially strong for both the onset and persistence of suicidal behavior, and the risk of suicidal behaviour is particularly high during childhood and adolescence, with the association between childhood adversities and suicidal behaviour decreasing with age. Traumatic life events throughout maturity, Unfortunately, bad life experiences may affect wellness at any age, and traumatic occurrences throughout adulthood (eg, physical or sexual abuse; loss of a loved one;

catastrophes or accidents; and exposure to war or other violence) can significantly raise the likelihood of eventual suicide conduct. Study findings have demonstrated a dose-response association between the number of forms of adversities and risk of eventual suicidal conduct; again, physical and sexual abuse appear to represent the greatest risk for both the initiation and persistence of suicidal behaviour.

Physical diseases have also been connected with suicidal behaviors. The presence and accumulation of physical illnesses (eg, heart disease, chronic pain, and respiratory disorders) are significantly associated with subsequent suicidal behaviour. The mechanism via which physical disease raises the risk of suicide behaviors is not known. Some research findings imply that this connection is linked to the presence of depression, however other investigators have observed that this association maintains even after adjusting for mental diseases. Other interpersonal pressures

Various forms of interpersonal stress may raise the likelihood of suicide conduct, even after adjusting for the effects of mental diseases.

Psychological treatment Most people struggling with suicidal thoughts and behaviours (roughly 60%) do not receive treatment. The main reasons for not seeking help are low perceived need and the desire to handle the problem personally. Future research is required to create effective approaches to link persons with suicide thoughts and behavior with effective therapies. Unfortunately, few well-established evidence-based therapies for suicidal conduct are available, such as preventative programmes, pharmacological interventions, and psycho logical treatments. Treatments targeting depression have not been shown to reduce suicidal thoughts or behaviours. Some evidence suggests that specific forms of cognitive and behavioural therapy that target suicidal thoughts and behaviours directly can decrease the risk of suicide reattempt among people who have made a previous attempt. For example, clinical trials testing dialectical behaviour therapy (in patients with a borderline personality disorder) and cognitive therapy (in recent suicide attempters) have lent support to the effectiveness of these treatments to reduce the rate of suicide reattempts compared

Safety-planning interventions, which include the identifi cation of warning signs, coping strategies, and sources of support in addition to the restriction of access to lethal means, are also receiving welcome attention. Treatment based on mentalization has shown some promise to reduce self-harm in adolescents. The fact that most suicidal persons do not get therapy, and that little evidence is available for the effectiveness of the interventions received by those who do, underscores the immense necessity of future efforts to create psychiatric therapies for those at risk of suicidal conduct. The usefulness of the internet and cell phones in treatment delivery also demands thorough consideration. Key areas for psychological research Despite tremendous gains in understanding the suicidal mentality, much more psychological study is required. Studies of suicide should routinely incorporate psychological components, especially in the case of large-scale national-linkage studies of suicide and suicide attempts. Psychological autopsy studies, in which information is collected about the deceased person from several informants, have played a key part in understanding the risk factors for suicide. More sophisticated autopsy studies in the future should be set up to investigate psychological factors in more detail. Research efforts to differentiate between suicide ideators, suicide attempters, and repeated attempters should be emphasized, since knowledge of the characteristics that permit or hinder behavioural enactment will influence the creation of intervention studies. Studies that leverage modern technology (eg, cellphones) and real-time data collecting (eg, ecological momentary assessment) are crucial in this respect. Focus on the differential effects of psychological aspects of suicide risk as a function of age, culture, and ethnic origin should be enhanced.

Chapter 4

Invalidating environment

Traumatic invalidation may undermine your self-worth and mental health. Healing is achievable via treatment and support.
It is wonderful to gain approval from others around us. This is when people acknowledge and confirm our emotions, experiences, and perspectives.
On the other side, it may hurt when you share your sentiments only to be ignored or informed that you're overexaggerating or lying. When you're invalidated by others around you, it may hurt your self-worth and impair your mental health.

Traumatic invalidation is when you're strongly or persistently invalidated by others around you. This may happen when your emotions, experiences, and memories are ignored or viewed as unacceptable.

Invalidation may be deliberate or not, but either way, it may create symptoms of post-traumatic stress when it's severe and frequent.
Although painful invalidation is frequently connected with childhood, adults may also suffer it.

What is traumatic invalidation?
Trauma is an emotional or physical reaction to one or more detrimental or life threatening events or situations having enduring unfavorable consequences on your mental and physical well-being, according to the Substance Abuse and Mental Health Services Administration (SAMSHA) (SAMSHA). Trauma may involve abuse, neglect, and accidents.

Invalidation may be painful when it is intense, long term, and adversely impacts your perception of yourself and the world. If you are constantly informed your emotions or experiences are illogical, you may be unable to accept your own emotional experiences. This might leave you feeling permanently uneasy.

An invalidating setting is one in which a young person does not feel recognized or supported.

This may be anything from a youngster receiving the message that certain feelings are unacceptable, to being told that they are incorrect, overreacting, are too sensitive and too demanding, or worst of all, that they are being manipulative.
For the Complex Trauma response to occur or for BPD to develop, invalidation has to occur over a period of time and from an early age. These invalidating events will also typically take place in the context of an attachment connection.

Children and young people are intrinsically more susceptible than adults and their

developmental requirements may create expectations and stressors on parents who may already be suffering hardship such as job loss, marital issues, financial troubles or personal crises.
Parents of course, may not want to be invalidating or to create distress, but for the developing kid, lack of emotional support and validation may be instantly stressful and may also produce more significant difficulties down the future.

Examples of painful invalidation include:

emotional abuse
verbal abuse
neglect being blamed while informing someone about a horrible incident or betrayal you encountered
Although this invalidation may come from anybody, it can be extremely upsetting from individuals who are close to you or those in positions of control over you.

Traumatic invalidation in childhood may result from several conditions, including:
A youngster informs their instructor that someone harmed or assaulted them. The instructor invalidates the child's experience by stating they're lying.
A youngster notifies their parents that they're unwell. Their parents accuse them of fake or exaggerating.
A youngster tears or tells their family they feel sad. Family members dismiss it as "hormonal mood swings," or punish them by stating "I'll give you something to weep about."
A person comes out to their parents as homosexual, trans, or queer. Their parents dismiss them or claim they're only going through a phase.

A parent who cannot tolerate unpleasant emotions can discourage them in their kid. For example, a mother advises her kid that talk of angry or sad thoughts will make him feel much worse. Instead of a futile discussion of sentiments, she argues, he should adopt a "positive attitude" and "get on with life" or "pull his socks up".

The parent opposes the child's account and interpretation of his own feelings and wishes. For example, a parent who informs his kid (after he shows the father a picture he has drawn) that there is no reason why he should feel so proud.

The parent has expectations that are too high for the developmental stage of the kid. She oversimplifies the process of problem-solving and downplays the hurdles. For example, a mother who tells her daughter (who is learning to tie her shoelaces) that she is taking too long and that even a foolish person would have figured it out by now.

A youngster could show outrage at her father's terrible behaviors. Her father then accuses her of faking her anger and having a secret goal.

Something that could also be heard in a setting like this is “you can’t possibly be (hungry, weary, upset, nervous etc)” or “don’t tell me that.”
Often the youngster will hide their actual sentiments in order to be accepted. Sometimes a facial expression or tone of voice is enough for a sensitive youngster to believe that their genuine self is undesired. Often the parents who are in circumstances such as those mentioned above are uncomfortable with emotion - their own and other people’s.

They may become uneasy or dismissive in the face of unexpected or powerful responses, frequently transferring their own anxieties onto their children, making it harder for the youngster to comprehend and regulate their own emotions.

Without support and acceptance for their growing self, the young kid will have difficulties evolving into someone with excellent self-esteem who knows and can effectively regulate their own emotional states.
If you are repeatedly informed that you are not experiencing what you are feeling, then you will be unable to acknowledge what is going on within you and will be at war with yourself, cling to others for self-definition or feel empty most of the time.

Examples of catastrophic invalidation in maturity include:

A Individual of Color person states that their co-worker regularly makes racist statements against them. Their coworkers and supervisor invalidate them by stating they're misinterpreting or exaggerating the statements.

A guy alleges that he has been physically mistreated by his girlfriend. The police refuse to aid him and declare that his experience isn't actually domestic abuse.

A lady comes out as transgender and says that she uses she her pronouns. Those around her disregard this and misgender her, using the improper pronouns or deadname.

A person with persistent pain seeks medical care. Doctors are dismissive and accuse patients of making up or exaggerating their symptoms.

Traumatic invalidation may be devastating in many ways. For one, it might educate someone to ignore or minimize their emotions or recollections. They may learn to think that their emotions shouldn't be believed.

When experiences of suffering and abuse are rejected, people may think that they shouldn't speak out when others mistreat them.

Where does invalidation originate from? Feelings of invalidation may frequently be traced back to childhood events. Whether purposefully or inadvertently, individuals around us could make us feel that our feelings, experiences, and memories are invalid. Feelings of invalidation might also arise from events you encountered as an adult.

Discrimination may have a factor in who is disqualified and why. People with a marginalized race, ethnicity, disability status, sexuality, or gender identity commonly experience discrimination. People's experiences with prejudice are often downplayed or dismissed, and their identities invalidated.

Communities that experience racism or discrimination based on their sexual or gender identity are also more likely to experience other forms of trauma.

Mental health Invalidation can have numerous harmful effects on your mental health. Traumatic invalidation is linked to mental health conditions, such as borderline personality disorder (BPD) and post-traumatic stress disorder (PTSD). Invalidation can also affect your physical health. A 2019 study found that people with chronic pain often experienced traumatic invalidation by others who disbelieve their symptoms. This could worsen symptoms and make it less likely for them to seek necessary medical help.

What you can do

Being invalidated isn't your fault. Although you did nothing to deserve it, there are things you can do to help yourself recover from the trauma of invalidation. Healing is possible.

This may involve counselling, which is an excellent technique to learn to deal in the aftermath of trauma. Many different forms of treatment may be used to manage trauma, including:

cognitive behavioral treatment (CBT) (CBT)
extended exposure (PE) (PE) therapy
trauma-focused CBT (TF-CBT) for children
Eye Movement Desensitization and Reprocessing (EMDR) (EMDR) therapy
psychodynamic therapy somatic experience (SE) (SE)
In addition to treatment, you may wish to explore the following:

Joining support groups that are relevant to your experience
Setting boundaries with people who invalidate or downplay your experiences
Finding healthy ways to relieve stress, such as exercise, meditation, and journaling.

Emotional Invalidation.

Emotional invalidation can be hurtful, but learning to recognize it might help prevent its effects.
Validation is the acceptance of a person's thoughts, feelings, and emotions. Invalidation, then, is just the opposite — when a person's thoughts, feelings, emotions, and behaviors are rejected, judged, or ignored.

Invalidation may impact anybody at any age, and whether you're a kid or adult, invalidation can be distressing and hurtful. Emotional invalidation from yourself or from others may frequently lead to feelings of worthlessness and self-isolation. These sentiments may then effect your day-to-day life – at work, at home, and in your relationships.
In certain circumstances, emotional invalidation may lead to additional unpleasant feelings and even mental health disorders. But it doesn't have to.

Understanding invalidation and learning how to detect it will help you learn to better cope with it when it comes.

What is emotional invalidation?
Emotional invalidation is the act of discounting or rejecting someone's beliefs, emotions, or actions. It conveys to someone: "Your sentiments don't matter. Your emotions are wrong."
Emotional invalidation might make you feel insignificant or illogical. It may take numerous forms and happen at any moment.
Some individuals use it purposely as a technique to control you by making you doubt your sentiments. They could remark something like: "I'm sure it wasn't really that bad."

Others could do it accidentally by attempting to cheer you up in a difficult circumstance. This can sound like:

"Everything occurs for a reason" or "It might be worse." Though this form of emotional invalidation is done by mistake with well-meaning intentions, it doesn't make it sting any less.

Emotional invalidation doesn't only have to be vocal, though.

It may also encompass nonverbal gestures like as rolling your eyes, ignoring the individual, or playing on your phone while someone is talking.

No matter how it occurs, emotional invalidation may engender uncertainty and mistrust.

Why do people invalidate?

Emotional invalidation typically arises while you're expressing your emotions or talking about an incident.

People frequently invalidate someone because they're unable to handle that person's feelings. They can be engrossed with their own issues or not know how to react at the moment.

Invalidation may also be used as an argument technique. It offers the illusion of supporting the way someone feels, while distancing or avoiding accepting responsibility for their involvement in those feelings.

Emotional invalidation may appear like blaming, name calling, and problem-solving before comprehending the other person's perspective. Playing down another person's experience is another technique to invalidate.

Emotional invalidation statements

It might be worse

You're overly sensitive You're overreacting you shouldn't feel that way

I know precisely how you feel

Just let it go

You take things so personally You make a huge issue out of everything I don't see the problem

You shouldn't be so [whatever sentiment the individual has voiced]
How do you think that makes me feel?
I don't want to have this conversation Stop making things up That didn't happen

Consequences of invalidation
Emotional invalidation may produce a variety of consequences:

Problems controlling emotions: Emotional invalidation may lead to perplexity, self-doubt, and skepticism in your own feelings. It indicates that your inner ideas and sensations are "wrong." With frequent exposure, you can grow to reject the veracity of your own personal experiences.
Issues with personal identity: People who believe their feelings are invalidated frequently suppress their emotions and develop poor self-esteem.
Mental health issues: Emotional invalidation may lead to someone having a mental health disorder, such as sadness and

anxiety. If you already have a mental health disorder, it can make your symptoms worse. While emotional invalidation may happen at any time in your life, if it occurs in childhood, it can have long-lasting impacts that can endure into adulthood. This is especially true for persons who feel emotions more profoundly than others.

There's some concern that emotional invalidation could lead to the development of borderline personality disorder (BPD) – a condition linked with instability in emotions, relationships, and self-image.

People afflicted with BPD often have:

difficulties controlling emotions
persistent sensations of emptiness
issues with self-image or sense of
self\srapidly shifting emotions
impulsiveness

As a youngster, you begin to learn and grasp how the world works. These lessons may impact the way you perceive the world, how you behave, the way you respond, and your thoughts and emotions.
Youngsters who are more “sensitive” could respond more intensely to particular circumstances or events than other children. If a kid grows up in an invalidating environment, they may not learn how to handle stress or control their emotions. Instead, individuals could learn how to mistrust their emotional reactions and suppress their sentiments.

Emotional validation

Validation informs someone that their feelings are valued. It creates room for another person’s feelings to exist. Through validation, we may affirm that others have their own emotional experiences and that those feelings are genuine, valuable, and essential.

So, how can you practice emotional validation?

The first step is to listen. Fully tune in to the debate. Put all distractions aside and dedicate your focus to the speaker.
It could also be useful to become familiar with phrases that are encouraging, compassionate, and that give space for all emotions throughout the talk.

Other ways you might prevent emotional invalidation is to:

avoid being defensive
not provide unwanted advice
take responsibility for the feeling when appropriate
Some validating sentences to try:

Instead of: Consider this:
"It might have been worse" "I'm so sorry that happened"

“That doesn’t sound too bad” “That must have been incredibly hard”
“You’ll get over it” “I care about you. What can I do to help?”
“I don’t want to hear it” “I’m here for you”
“You’re overreacting” “That sounds frustrating”
“Don’t be such a crybaby” “I can see you’re really upset”
“What’s the big deal?” “This must be so painful”

Navigating relationships is far from straightforward. But being more aware of the language you use in conversations can make a real difference.
Learning to recognize invalidating behaviors and statements can help you develop a healthier relationship with others and yourself.

Chapter 6

Suicide techniques

A suicide technique in any manner by which a person decides to terminate their life. Suicide attempts may not always end in death, and a nonfatal suicide attempt can leave the victim with major physical injuries, long-term health issues, and brain damage.
Worldwide, three suicide techniques prevail with the pattern differing in various nations. These are hanging, poisoning by chemicals, and weapons.

Some suicides are spontaneous judgments that may be avoidable by eliminating the means. Making popular suicide techniques less available leads to an overall drop in the number of suicides. Some strategies to achieve this include limiting access to pesticides, guns, and known-used narcotics. Other essential initiatives include the adoption of laws that address the usage of alcohol and the treatment of mental problems. Gun-control measures in several countries have seen a reduction in suicides and other gun-related deaths.

Method restriction

Method limitation, often termed deadly means reduction, is an efficient approach to minimize the number of suicide fatalities in the short and medium term. Method limitation is considered a best practice backed by "compelling" evidence. Some of these efforts, such as building barriers on bridges and decreasing the toxicity of gas, require action by governments, companies, or public utilities. At the individual level, method limitation may be as easy as requesting a trusted friend or family member to keep weapons until the crisis has passed. Choosing not to limit access to suicide techniques is deemed immoral.

Method limitation is beneficial and avoids suicides. It has the most influence on overall suicide rates when the technique being prohibited is prevalent and no direct alternative is available. If the technique being limited is infrequent, or if an alternative is easily accessible, then it may be beneficial in individual situations but not create a large-scale decrease in the number of fatalities in a country.

Method substitution is the process of choosing a different suicide method when the first-choice method is inaccessible. In many circumstances, when the first-choice technique is constrained, the individual does not seek to locate an alternative. Method substitution has been studied over decades, so when a popular method is limited (for example, by making household gas less lethal), total suicide rates may be lowered for many years. If the first-choice suicide technique is unavailable, a method substitute may be performed which may be less harmful, and likely to result in fewer fatal suicide attempts.

In an example of the curb-cut effect, modifications unrelated to suicide have also functioned as suicide method limits. Examples of this include improvement to align train doors with platforms, moving from coal gas to natural gas in residences, and gun control legislation, all of which have decreased suicides while being intended for a different goal.

Suffocation

Suicide by suffocation includes reducing breathing or the quantity of oxygen taken in, creating asphyxia, and finally hypoxia. It is not possible to die solely by holding the breath, as a reflex leads the respiratory muscles to contract, forcing an in-breath, and the re-establishment of a regular breathing rhythm. Therefore, breathing an inert gas such as helium or nitrogen, or a harmful gas such as carbon monoxide, is employed to bring about unconsciousness. As of 2010, organizations supporting a right to die promoted death by helium inhalation, although most cases using this method in the US where people with psychiatric conditions.

Hanging

Hanging is a prevalent form of suicide. The hanging includes the use of a ligature such as a rope or cord tied to an anchor point with the other end users to make a noose put around the neck. The cause of death will either be due to strangling or a fractured neck. About half of attempted suicides by hanging result in death. People who like this approach are frequently ignorant that it is often a "slow, unpleasant, and untidy process that [requires] technical understanding"

Hanging is the typical way of suicide in poor pre-industrial communities and is more frequent in rural regions than in metropolitan ones. It is also a typical form of suicide in contexts when other materials are not easily accessible, such as in prisons.

Hanging was the most prevalent technique in old Chinese society, since it was thought that the wrath involved in such a death caused the person's ghost to visit and afflict survivors. In the Chinese culture, suicide by hanging was employed as an act of retribution by women and of defiance by helpless officials, who used it as a "final, but unmistakable, manner of standing still against and above tyrannical rulers". Chinese people would typically approach the rite ceremonially, including the usage of formal clothes.

Poisoning

Suicide by poisoning, often termed self-poisoning, is typically categorised as a drug overdose when medications such as painkillers or recreational substances are used. The use of pesticides to self-poison is

the most popular approach utilized in several nations. Poisoning by the methods of hazardous plants is typically gradual and painful.
As of 2006, globally, roughly 30% of suicides were from pesticide poisonings. The adoption of this approach varies greatly in various parts of the globe, from 0.9% in Europe to over 50% in the Pacific region.] In the US, pesticide poisoning is utilized in roughly 12 suicides every year.

Method limitation has proven a successful strategy to minimize suicide by poisoning in several nations. In Finland, limiting access to parathion in the 1960s resulted in a rapid decline in both poisoning-related suicides and total suicide deaths for several years, and a slower decline in subsequent years. In Sri Lanka, both suicide by pesticide and total suicides declined after first toxicity class I and later class II endosulfan were banned. Overall suicide deaths were cut by 70%, with 93,000 lives saved over 20 years as a result of banning these pesticides. In Korea, banning a single pesticide, paraquat, cut the rate of suicides by pesticide poisoning and lowered the overall number of suicides in that nation.

Drug overdose

A drug overdose entails consuming a dosage of a substance that exceeds safe limits. Among the UK until 2013, a drug overdose was the most prevalent suicide method in females. Among 2019 in men the proportion is 16%. Self-poisoning accounts for the biggest number of non-fatal suicide attempts. Overdose attempts with painkillers are among the most prevalent, given to their simple availability over-the-counter. Paracetamol is the most extensively used painkiller globally and is regularly used in overdose attempts. Paracetamol poisoning is a frequent cause of acute liver failure. In the United States roughly 60% of suicide attempts and 14% of suicide fatalities include drug overdoses.

The probability of fatality in suicide attempts involving overdose is roughly 2%.

Carbon monoxide

A specific kind of poisoning includes the intake of excessive quantities of carbon monoxide (CO) (CO). Death frequently happens from hypoxia. A nonfatal attempt might result in memory loss and other problems.

Carbon monoxide is a colorless and odorless gas, therefore its presence cannot be detected by sight or smell. It functions by binding preferentially to the hemoglobin in the circulation, displacing oxygen molecules and steadily deoxygenating the blood, finally leading in the failure of cellular respiration and death. Carbon monoxide is exceedingly deadly to onlookers and anybody who may find the corpse; right-to-die advocate Philip Nitschke has consequently cautioned against this procedure.

Before air quality standards and catalytic converters, suicide by carbon monoxide poisoning was typically performed by running a car's engine in an enclosed location such as a garage, or by diverting a running car's exhaust back into the cabin using a hose. Motor vehicle exhaust may have had up to 25% carbon monoxide. Catalytic converters installed on all current autos reduce over 99% of carbon monoxide generated. As an additional difficulty, the quantity of unburned gasoline in emissions may make exhaust uncomfortable to breathe long before a person loses consciousness. Charcoal-burning suicide promotes death from carbon monoxide poisoning. Originally employed in Hong Kong, it migrated to Japan, where tiny charcoal-burning heaters (hibachi) or stoves (shichirin) have been utilized in a sealed space. Nonfatal attempts may result in significant brain damage owing to cerebral anoxia.

Other poisons
Household gas was initially coal gas, sometimes called illuminating gas, or town gas, which was made of methane, hydrogen and carbon monoxide. Stoves of this era required one to manually ignite a pilot light with a match; without the combustion the gas cloud would spread unimpeded.

Shooting

Comparison of gun-related suicide rates versus non-gun-related suicide rates in high-income OECD nations, 2010, countries in graph arranged by total suicides. The US was the only OECD nation in which gun suicide rates surpassed non-gun suicide rates.
In the United States suicide by firearm is the most dangerous mode of suicide, resulting in a fatality 90% of the time, and is therefore the primary cause of death by suicide as of 2017. Worldwide, firearm prevalence in suicides varies greatly, depending on the acceptability and availability of weapons in a

society. The usage of guns in suicides varies from less than 10% in Australia to 50.5% in the U.S., where it is the most prevalent form of suicide.

Generally, the bullet will be targeted at point-blank range. Surviving a self-inflicted gunshot may result in significant chronic pain as well as impaired cognitive capacities and motor function, subdural hematoma, foreign things in the brain, pneumocephalus and cerebrospinal fluid leakage. For temporal bone aimed bullets, temporal lobe abscess, meningitis, aphasia, hemianopsia, and hemiplegia are typical late intracranial consequences. As many as 50% of persons who survive gunshot wounds aimed at the temporal bone have facial nerve injury, generally owing to a severed nerve.

Jumping

In the United States, jumping is among the least common methods of suicide. In a 75-year span through 2012, there were roughly 1,400 suicides along the Golden Gate Bridge. In New Zealand, security fencing at the Grafton Bridge drastically lowered the number of suicides.

Jumping is the most prevalent means of suicide in Hong Kong, accounting for 52.1% of all recorded suicide cases in 2006 and comparable proportions for the years preceding that. The Centre for Suicide Research and Prevention at the University of Hong Kong argues that it may be linked to the presence of readily accessible high-rise buildings in Hong Kong.

Jumping fatalities may frequently be averted with the building of fence or other safety infrastructure. For example, suicide by leaping into a volcano crater is an uncommon way of suicide. Mount Mihara in Japan temporarily became a known suicide location during the Great Depression after media reports of a suicide there. Copycat suicides in the coming years spurred the building of a protective fence encircling the crater.

Cutting and stabbing

A fatal self-inflicted wound to the wrist is termed a deep wrist injury, and is often preceded by several tentative surface-breaking attempts known as hesitation wounds, indicating indecision or a self-harm tactic. For every suicide by wrist cutting, there are many more nonfatal attempts, such that the number of real fatalities using this technique is quite low.

Wounds from suicide attempts affect the non-dominant hand, with damage commonly done to the median nerve, ulnar nerve, radial artery, palmaris longus muscle, and flexor carpi radialis muscle. Such injuries may seriously limit the function of the hand, and the incapacity induced to carry out job or hobbies raises the danger of additional attempts.

Seppuku is a kind of Japanese ceremonial suicide by disembowelment. It was traditionally designated for samurai in their code of honour. It is not widely used in the present day since it is unpleasant and slow.

Drowning

Suicide by drowning is the act of deliberately submerging oneself in water or other liquid to prevent breathing. It accounts for fewer than 2% of all suicides in the United States. Of those who attempt suicide by drowning in the US, about half die.

Starvation and dehydration

A categorization has been created of Voluntary Stopping Eating and Drinking (VSED) which is commonly resorted to in terminal sickness. This involves hunger and dehydration, and has also been referred to as autoeuthanasia.
Fasting to death has been used by Hindu, Buddhist, and Jain ascetics and

householders, as a ritual method of suicide known as Prayopavesa in Hinduism; Sokushinbutsu historically in Buddhism; and as Sallekhana in Jainis Cathars also fasted to death after receiving the consolamentum sacrament, in order to die while in a morally perfect state. This type of death is also related with the political protest of the hunger strike such as the 1981 Irish hunger strike in which 10 inmates died.
Death from dehydration might take from several days to a few weeks. This implies that unlike many other suicide techniques, it cannot be completed spontaneously. Those who die by terminal dehydration often go into unconsciousness before death, and may also have delirium and disordered serum sodium.

Terminal dehydration has been regarded as having major benefits over physician-assisted suicide with regards to self-determination, access, professional ethics, and societal repercussions. Specifically, a patient has a right to refuse treatment and it would be a personal assault for someone to force water on a patient, but such is not the case if a doctor merely refuses to provide lethal medication. But it also has distinctive drawbacks as a humane means of voluntary death. One poll of hospice nurses indicated that almost twice as many had cared for patients who chose voluntary rejection of food and water to accelerate death as had cared for patients who selected physician-assisted suicide. They also evaluated starvation and dehydration as causing less suffering and agony and being more calm than physician-assisted death. Other sources describe severely unpleasant adverse effects of dehydration, including seizures, skin breaking and bleeding, blindness, nausea, vomiting, cramps and severe headaches.

Collision with or of a vehicle

Another suicide option is to lay down, or fling oneself, in the path of a fast-moving vehicle, either on the road or onto railway lines. Nonfatal attempts may result in profound injuries, such as multiple bone fractures, amputations, concussion and severe mental and physical handicapping. Some people use intentional car crashes as a suicide method. This especially applies to single-occupant, single-vehicle wrecks, although some suicidal people cause head-on collisions with heavier vehicles. Even single-vehicle collisions may harm other road users; for example, a driver who brakes abruptly or swerves to avoid a suicidal person may collide with something else on the road, resulting in harm to the driver or others. Both the intended motorist and spectators may be traumatized by the encounter, even if everyone escapes.

Air

Toward the end of the 20th century, one or two pilots in the US died by suicide via plane per year. The pilot was frequently flying alone at the time, and was using alcohol or drugs around half the time. In the rare occurrence of a pilot participating in murder–suicide, the number of innocent individuals is occasionally quite high. On 24 March 2015, a Germanwings co-pilot intentionally crashed Germanwings Flight 9525 into the French Alps to kill himself, killing 150 passengers with him. Suicide by pilot has also been offered as a plausible explanation for the disappearance and ensuing destruction of Malaysian Airlines Flight 370 in 2014, with corroborating evidence being discovered in an aircraft simulator program used by the flight's pilot.

Disease

There have been documented cases of gay men deliberately trying to contract a disease such as HIV/AIDS as a means of suicide.

Electrocution

Suicide by electrocution involves using a lethal electric shock, and is a rarely used method.

[133] This produces arrhythmias of the heart, meaning that the heart does not contract in synchrony across the separate chambers, effectively causing elimination of blood flow. Furthermore, depending on the current, burns may also occur. In his opinion outlawing the electric chair as a method of execution, Justice William M. Connolly of the Nebraska Supreme Court stated that "electrocution inflicts intense pain and agonizing suffering", adding that it is "unnecessarily cruel in its purposeless infliction of physical violence and mutilation of the prisoner's body."

Fire

Self-immolation is suicide generally by fire. This method of suicide is rare due to its being long and painful. If the attempt is intervened, severe burns and scar tissue will prevail with subsequent emotional impact. It has been used as a protest tactic, by Thích Quảng Đức in 1963 to protest the South Vietnam's anti-Buddhist policies; by Malachi Ritscher in 2006 to protest the United States' involvement in the Iraq War; by Mohamed Bouazizi in 2011 in Tunisia which gave rise to the Tunisian Revolution; and historically as a ritual known as sati where a Hindu widow would immolate herself in her husband's funeral pyre.

Hypothermia

Hypothermia is an extremely rare method of suicide. As of 2015, there have been only nine cases in the scientific literature.

Assisted suicide

Indirect suicide is the act of setting out on an obviously fatal course without directly carrying out the act upon oneself. Indirect suicide is differentiated from legally defined suicide by the fact that the person does not directly cause the action meant to kill them, but rather expects and allows the action to happen to them. Examples of indirect suicide include a soldier enlisting in the army with the intention and expectation of being killed in combat, or provoking an armed law enforcement officer into using lethal force against them. The latter is typically labeled "suicide by policeman".

Evidence exists for suicide by capital crime in colonial Australia. Convicts seeking to escape their brutal treatment would murder another individual. This was thought essential owing to a religious taboo against direct suicide. A person completing suicide was believed to be destined for hell, whereas a person committing murder could be absolved of their sins before execution. In its most extreme form, groups of prisoners on the extremely brutal penal colony of Norfolk Island would form suicide lotteries. Prisoners would draw straws with one prisoner murdering another. The remaining participants would witness the crime, and would be sent away to Sydney, as capital trials could not be held on Norfolk Island, thus earning a break from the Island. There is uncertainty as to the extent of suicide lotteries. While surviving contemporaneous reports indicate that the practice was prevalent, such statements are probably overblown.

Rituals:
Ritual suicide is performed in a prescribed way, usually involving fasting, and often as part of a religious or cultural practice. Seppuku, also known as harakiri, is a medieval Japanese ceremonial suicide procedure involves inflicting a serious wound to the belly.

Chapter 7

Intellectual and spiritual change

Historically, and still today in some locations, suicide is considered a criminal offense, a religious taboo, and, in some cases, an act of honor (e.g., kamikaze and suicide bombing) In a multi-faith and multicultural world, psychiatrists and other mental health professionals are confronted by distressed patients for whom religious beliefs shape psychopathological symptoms and their compliance with treatment. Therefore, religious and spiritual aspects should be considered in the context of the patient's mental diagnosis and also taken into consideration in the process of determining the right psychiatric therapy.

Initially, I thought of suicide as a loss of significance for the person, while spirituality was possibly a search or quest to rediscover some purpose in life. But how does it tie in with the many religions and cultures? I thought, of course, of the suicide bombers and the attitude of Islam and Christianity towards suicide. My understanding is that Islam esteems the human being as high as Christianity. Life is considered a gift from God and the person is accountable to God for how he utilizes it. Because life is holy, taking one's own life is forbidden except in self-defense.

The Jihad (which does not imply Holy Conflict) as applied to war is purely\sdefensive. If Islamic land, people, or property is taken, Muslims must 'fight against those who battle against you. The regulations are fairly clear. Only combatants may be assaulted. No persons, no business, or agricultural property may be injured. Muslims have a considerably stronger idea of themselves as a collective, with less stress on the independent person, than we in the West. Israel provides a difficult issue. The Islamic land stolen from the Palestinians is occupied and held by 'civilians' who have created business and agricultural operations on it. Are these citizens then actively collaborating in the injustice and are they consequently susceptible to violence done to them to reject their occupation? How one answers this question either legitimise or condemns the suicide bombers. 'No peace without justice' stated Pope Paul VI before the UN. The Palestinians are treated terribly by Israel; they are 3rd class citizens in their nation. They are violated and discriminated against in every way. The kids have no hope. On an individual Palestinian level, this is a prescription for suicide. On a societal level, it is a ripe opportunity for fundamentalists, who appear to give a clear answer to the problems of the hopeless person and the dismal community. Durkheim showed us that most commonly it is the least integrated members of a society who commit suicide.

There is no question that some political and fundamentalist groups, such as Al Qa'ida, seek out impressionable young men, indoctrinate them and send them on suicide missions; this is the cost associated with a culture of high social solidarity and group identification versus an individualistic one. Thus it would seem that for the suicide bombers the purpose of their death is a desire to sacrifice themself for the greater welfare of their community, an altruistic suicide.

The Christian church has a long history of condemning suicide.

places suicide and murder in the same category of sin. In 'Wood of Suicides' human the shapes have been converted into trees, which scream out with anguish as bleeding branches are cut off.

However, 75% of the suicides have provided some type of warning and if they have tried previously they are 3 times as likely to attempt again.

Total loneliness is a precursor of suicidal depression.

I quote: ‘once a guy chooses to end his life he enters a sealed off, impenetrable yet wholly believable universe where every detail matches and each occurrence strengthens his decision. A dispute at a bar, the incorrect voice on the telephone, even a change in the weather - all appear imbued with a specific significance; they all contribute.

So it is the person’s perspective or interpretation of the environment around them that\scan decides their behavior.

I have two instances when an outside influence affected the person’s viewpoint.

Denis had cooked a fatal cake and had begun to devour it when a postcard arrived in his mailbox. It came from his mother who he had not been in touch with for 5 years. It stated, ’every cloud has a silver lining’.

Denis then rang for an ambulance.

Ian had climbed onto Battersea Bridge. He had just completed his bottle of vodka and was prepared to leap. A guy went by and asked him if he needed a push. Ian was so upset at this seeming callousness that climbed back over to confront the guy. I am not proposing this as a method but possibly in this situation, the man succeeded in deflecting the wrath that Ian had put against himself.

Pascal viewed human beings as wretched because of their unmet needs, the vacuum at the heart of their being, which they frantically attempt to ignore by ceaseless activity and seeking pleasure. Baudelaire was a guy without a core. He inherited a Catholic conscience without the religion and was afflicted by a feeling of guilt and consequent self-hatred. He was a classic narcissist, who only saw the external world mirrored in his ego. Sartre stated he never grew up and remained in a perpetual condition of immaturity. He sought to escape the loneliness with sex, drugs, and art. He wrote, 'to desire nothing, to feel nothing, to sleep and carry on sleeping, that today is my sole wish. Ignoble and vile want but sincere', and, 'I dread sleep as one fears a huge pit, full of impending terror, leading one does not know whither. I can see nothing but the limitless through every window.'

Sartre explains the hopelessness. 'A cursed man walking without a lantern down the brink of an abyss whose stench reveals its moist depth, down interminable stairs without banisters, where slimy creatures wait, whose enormous phosphorescent eyes make the night darker still and leave nothing visible but themselves.'

The terror of the emptiness of life and the emptiness in the human heart brings a longing for the termination of existence. But the endless nothingness has another side to it - humanity's limitless longings for pleasure, satisfaction, for beauty. There was a genuine desire in Sartre to fulfill the limitless craving of his human heart. These idealized longings were eventually disappointed. Thus the frustration of the latter was the cause of the 'bottomless pit.

Of course, self-harm may have different connotations beyond the want to die. If we look to the past in Christianity, mortification of the body has typically been an important concept. For example, via flagellation, the body is punished, particularly for sexual urges, and by fasting, the body is controlled. Cross recounts the seriously skewed eating habits among 'the Holy Women' of Medieval Europe, noting that these women who exercised rigorous fasting and cleansing of their bodies earned social respect and even authority. She points out that this is in sharp contrast to the impotent self-destruction of the current anorexic and self-cutting women.

I am dealing with a patient at the moment who has had three of her circle of friends commit suicide in the previous six months. She answered, 'It does become a possibility all of a sudden. They aren't suffering any longer, they don't have to keep dealing with this horrible world'

She went on to discuss her burial in some detail and got rather affronted when I remarked she appeared to want to stay around after her death. In reality, we came to realize that she wanted the broken part of her to die so that the healthier half may develop.

Tacey speaks on 'rites of passage', referring to mental shifts at key stages of our lives. He says suicide is a rite of passage gone awry. He thinks that\ssuicide is not logical and that there is a spiritual component, which is generally hidden from human understanding. He leans on his interaction with Aboriginal Elders to develop his idea. He argues we all have two identities, the ego, or first self, and the soul, or second self. The initial self is not first in importance but we learn about it first, before we find the deeper, more concealed self. The ego defines itself in terms of personal likes and dislikes, social adaptability, and connectivity with the outside world. The soul is concerned with different connectivity. It wants to feel linked with Spirit, the universe, and the planet. It is not nurtured by social status or financial success, but rather by meaning, worth, and purpose. The soul requires meaning that derives from a link to transcendental ideals. The soul's origin, according to Greek philosophy and most world religions, is transcendent, and only feels at home in this world to the degree that it is connected with the transcendent source. When a crisis arises the soul is exposed. Tacey says it is unreasonable for 'rational society to disregard the existence of the soul. We teach the mind and the intellect but not the heart and emotions.

The soul has always been the domain of religion, but in our more secular culture, the power of religion has been eroded. He refers to the paradox that just as society grows better in so many ways, we are burdened with dreadful mental health issues.

The admission into the spirit is ritualized in the form of initiations. The Aboriginal culture helps the individual through the transition; it ritualizes the grief and shares it with the community. It is a technique of controlling the agony of the loss and providing closure, before enjoying the next chapter. My understanding is that the purpose is to match the inner experience with the outside one. Tacey questioned an Aboriginal elder why so many young people are now killing themselves. He replied, 'they don't know who they are.'
Society no longer initiates us to the level it once did, but the human soul goes through its cycle of change - changes that are both biological and spiritual. But we are not addressing the spiritual requirements. In tribal culture, society supplies a vision for the individual. In the West, we want to have the flexibility to find our meanings. Any civilization without intelligence is living a lie. An Aboriginal Elder observed, 'you white

fellas are strange people, to us, it appears like you are not initiated'.

Tacey contends that we require symbolic thinking and knowledge for the spiritual part of our impulses to be achieved.

It is not unexpected that generosity is at the core of all excellent spiritual traditions and supports the notion of good conquering evil. It appears to me that both selves, the ego, and the soul, have to engage with each other, just as in our job we are aware of the interactions between the id, the ego, and the superego. Pascal concludes that reason must keep quiet, so that human beings may learn via revelations, the nature of their actual position. St John of the Cross sees the emptying of the mind of all knowledge and the emptying of all desire as a necessity to connect with God. The Mystical experience cannot be adequately articulated in words. (The closest analog is climaxing while making love).

Brendan Smith regards love as the breath of life. He contends that real love means acknowledging the evil side, the 'sin' within us, and attempting not to act it out. For those who disdain organized religion, it is consequently that the 'good' is symbolized as 'God'. Others could consider the concept of God as an idealized projection, part of infantile longings, or a return to the womb. Whatever one's views it appears to me that it is acknowledged that the 'good' and the 'bad' have to become merged for a person to become entire.

One thing I do want to raise - and I don't want to be regarded as idealizing religion. There is a possible conflict. We simply have to look at history to see that religion, like everything else, can be a source of evil as well as good. Formalized religion has frequently been the cause of dread and shame, not fostering love and understanding. I have been lucky; that has not been my own experience.

However other sufferers could perceive religion as a source of agony not healing. As therapists, I merely urge us to be aware of

the spiritual component and how it could connect to our patients.
And what about the 'ego's' basic self-needs? Joy in helping and relating to others (as we must know of ourselves) is an emotion that is felt not only by Taoist and Hindu sages, by Hebrew, Christian, and Muslim prophets but also by millions of anonymous humans, many of them atheists. Studies of people who are happier about their lives point to two factors; close stable relationships with others and involvement in their community. That is only the overt reason and it is always more complex. However, it does indicate a loss and an inability to love both others and themselves. I do think that connectedness makes individuals feel alive, and that applies both inside and outside. It is our inner resources that determine how we cope with the world and we ignore the spiritual dimension at our peril. As we try to help our patients develop their inner resources we always need to keep the spiritual dimension in mind.

Chapter 8
Prevention and treatment

The most identified risk factors for suicide are mental problems, genetics, drug addiction, and familial and societal conditions. Oftentimes, mental issues and drug misuse co-exist. Access to guns and other ways of suicide can increase the danger. For example, rates of suicide in houses with firearms are larger than in homes without them.

Mental problems have an overwhelming influence on the increased risk of suicide—with estimates estimating up to 90% of those who take their own life suffer from some sort of mental condition. The risk of suicide for those suffering from mental problems substantially lowers once accepted to therapy. The mental conditions having the largest prevalence of suicide risk linked with them are major depressive disorder, bipolar disorder, schizophrenia, personality disorders, post-traumatic stress disorder, and eating disorders. Individuals suffering from severe depressive illness and bipolar disorder are at the greatest risk of suicide—with the risk of suicide rising 20-fold.

Behind severe depressive illness and bipolar disorder, drug addiction ranked as the second-highest risk factor for suicide. Statistics reveal that drinking is prevalent at the time of death in up to 61% of completed suicide cases. Heroin and cocaine usage is also a prevalent risk factor for suicide, with heroin users having a 14-fold increased risk of suicide and cocaine users having a higher risk of suicide following withdrawal drug use. Cannabis usage has not been demonstrated to enhance suicide risk among users.

Genetics is assumed to have a factor in the risk of suicide—such that a family history of suicide tends to imply an increased risk of suicide among other family members—accounting for up to 55% of suicidal actions. A family history of mental problems and drug misuse is also a risk factor for suicide. In a similar sense, exposure to suicide (e.g., seeing a family member commit themselves or discovering their corpse) is likewise predictive of an elevated risk of suicidal behavior.

Family and socio-economic issues are also significant factors in suicide risk. Unemployment, homelessness, poverty, childhood sexual abuse, social isolation, the death of a loved one, and other life difficulties may all raise the chance of suicide. Sexual abuse alone is considered to contribute to 20% of the total risk of suicide.

EPIDEMIOLOGY OF SUICIDE

According to the CDC, general data on suicide include the following:
Every day, roughly 105 Americans die due to suicide
Overall suicide rates climbed 28% from 2000 to 2015
One person dies by suicide every 12.3 minutes in the United States
There is one completed suicide for every 25 attempted suicide attempts
In the elderly, there is one suicide for every 4 attempted suicide attempts
In the United States, rates of suicide are greatest among Whites, American Indians, and Alaska Natives

Gender Differences

Males are four times as likely than females to commit suicide
Females are more prone to experience thoughts of suicide

Females are four times as likely than men to attempt suicide
Males are more likely to use weapons to commit suicide
Females are more likely to employ poisons to commit suicide

Age Differences
1 in 100,000 youngsters aged 10 to 14 die by suicide each year
7 in 100,000 teenagers aged 15 to 19 die by suicide each year
12.7 in 100,000 young people aged 20 to 24 die by suicide per year

Symptoms
Often, but not always, a person may display specific indicators and behaviors preceding a suicide attempt, such as:

Having difficulties focusing or thinking clearly

Giving away belongings
Talking about moving away or the necessity to "get my things in order"
Suddenly altering demeanor, notable tranquility after a time of worry
Losing interest in things they used to like
Self-destructive activities, such as excessively consuming alcohol, taking illicit substances or slashing their body
Pulling away from friends or not wanting to go out
Suddenly having problems in school or work
talking about death or suicide, or even declaring that they wish to injure themselves
Talking about feeling hopeless or sorry
Changing sleep or eating habits
Arranging means killing their own life (such as getting a pistol or several pills) (such as buying a gun or many pills)

Not all persons with depression will display all symptoms or experience them to the same degree. If a person experiences four or more symptoms, for more than two weeks, visit a doctor or mental health expert straight once. While the symptoms described for all groups often define severe depression, there are other conditions with comparable features including bipolar illness, anxiety disorder, or attention deficit disorder with or without hyperactivity.

PREVENTION

Avoiding alcohol and drugs (other than prescription treatments) may lower the chance of suicide.
In houses with children or teenagers:

Keep any prescription drugs high up and secured.

Do not store alcohol in the house, or keep it locked away.
Do not store firearms in the house. If you do store weapons in the house, lock them and keep the ammunition separate.
In elderly individuals, further analyze emotions of despair, being a burden, and not belonging.

Many people try to take their own lives to speak about it before attempting it. Sometimes, simply talking to someone who cares and who does not criticize them is enough to lessen the risk of suicide. However, whether you are a friend or family member, or you know someone who you fear may attempt suicide, never try to handle the situation on your own.

Never overlook a suicide threat or attempted suicide.

Suicide prevention strategies and therapy are based on patient risk factors.

Treatments are provided in light of underlying illnesses in addition to avoidance of suicidal thoughts and behaviors. If you are suffering from a mental problem, a treatment strategy to manage this disease is executed initially. One of the most frequent suicide prevention strategies is psychotherapy— often known as talk therapy —in the form of Cognitive Behavioral Therapy (CBT) or Dialectical Behavior Therapy (DBT) (DBT).

Cognitive Behavioral Therapy is a prominent therapy choice for those suffering from a range of mental problems. In this form of psychotherapy, you are taught new methods of coping with stress and difficult life circumstances. In this method, when thoughts of suicide emerge, you may divert those ideas and deal with them in a different way than trying to end your own life.
Dialectical Behavior Therapy is intended to assist a person to identify disruptive or

harmful thoughts or behaviors. In connection, this therapeutic style then teaches skills on how to cope with challenging or troublesome circumstances. More study is required on psychotherapy linked to suicide prevention nevertheless, since DBT, in particular, has been demonstrated to lower the incidence of attempted suicide but has shown no impact on completed suicides.

Drugs may also be provided as a preventative technique to suicide; however, disagreement remains in this method, since many medications used in the treatment of mental problems involve an increased risk of suicide as a side effect. Antidepressants specifically entail a risk of a possible rise in suicidal thoughts and behavior—but this risk can be based on age. Clinical study has revealed that young people increase their risk of suicide and suicidal thoughts while using antidepressants, whereas, in older persons, this negative effect reduces.

Increased awareness among physicians is also a preventative approach. Research reveals that many persons who have committed suicide or attempted suicide did seek medical assistance in the year previous; nevertheless, warning indications may have been ignored. Increased knowledge and awareness among medical professionals could lower suicide rates in the future.

Popular "crisis hotlines" have not gotten reliable data signals in the study that imply their usage is useful or not. Though, one beneficial side effect of these hotlines is that they are often well-known which enhances the general population's awareness of suicide. In an extra attempt to promote awareness of suicide and risk factors connected with suicide, September 10 has been marked as World Suicide Prevention Day in conjunction with the International Association for Suicide Prevention and the World Health Organization.

Strengthen economic supports
Create protected habitats
Reduce access to fatal methods among those at risk of suicide.
Community involvement activities
Teach coping and problem-solving skills
Parenting skill and family relationship programs

TREATMENT

Friends and relatives may give all the assistance that is required in moderate episodes of depression. Having someone ready to listen and ask concerned questions may make all the difference. However, even the most loving and committed friends or family members may not be enough when depression is more severe. In such instances, it is vital to seek expert aid.

Mental health experts that may be consulted include psychiatrists, clinical psychologists, and masters-level therapists. Some may initially seek advice from a general physician or religious counselor. Each sort of professional has its viewpoint and skill, and practitioners of all types have experience dealing with depression. The main thing is to get expert care when symptoms are severe and/or prolonged. It is advisable to get care even when symptoms are not severe to help avoid depression from growing worse.

Some mild and most severe depressions respond to antidepressant medicines. These are given by a clinician, often a psychiatrist, following a comprehensive examination. A good impact is generally noticed within a few weeks. Some forms of mood disorders need specialized drugs; for example, persons with bipolar illness frequently do well on lithium. Taking medication does not prevent other types of therapy. Individual psychotherapy, alone or in conjunction with medication, is frequently useful. Insight-oriented psychotherapy tries to improve insight and awareness of unconscious conflicts, desires, and difficulties with the belief that greater knowledge would lead to more freedom to cope with concerns and a stronger sense of self. Other treatments use a cognitive and/or behavioral approach and aim to modify harmful habits of thinking or address isolation by helping the client build interpersonal skills. Group therapy has been demonstrated to be useful in managing depression symptoms and developing insights about the self and connections to others.

Therapists may assist people to make adjustments in tough life circumstances. With the individual's agreement, they may arrange sessions with friends or parents to discuss options for resolving a problem. Depressed persons who are at high risk of harming themselves may need to stay in a hospital temporarily. While this may seem like an extreme move, it may be life-saving, and it may enable the individual to obtain the therapy and assistance that they need.

People who are at risk of suicide conduct may not seek therapy for several reasons, including:

They feel nothing will help.
They do not want to inform anybody they have troubles.
They believe asking for aid is a sign of weakness.
They do not know where to go for assistance.
They feel their loved ones would be better off without them.
A person may require emergency care following a suicide attempt. They may need first aid, CPR, or more intensive treatments.

People who try to take their own life may need to stay in a hospital for treatment and to reduce the risk of future attempts. Therapy is one of the most important parts of treatment.

Treatment of suicidal thoughts and behavior depends on your specific situation, including your level of suicide risk and what underlying problems may be causing your suicidal thoughts or behavior.
If you are suicidal, call the National Suicide Prevention Lifeline at 1-800-273-TALK (8255), available 24 hours a day, 7 days a week. Anyone may call toll-free and all calls are confidential. Or, just phone or text 988 to contact the crisis helpline.

If you know of someone who is suicidal, do not leave the individual alone. Attempt to get them quick care from their medical professional, hospital, or phone 911. Remove access to harmful objects, such as weapons, medicines, or other possible threats.

Your doctor may want you to remain in the hospital long enough to make sure any therapies are working, that you'll be safe when you leave and that you'll receive the follow-up therapy you need.

Nonemergency circumstances

If you have suicidal thoughts but aren't in a crisis scenario, you may require outpatient care. This therapy may include:

Psychotherapy. In psychotherapy, also called psychological counseling or talk therapy, you explore the issues that make you feel suicidal and learn skills to help manage emotions more effectively. You and your therapist can work together to develop a treatment plan and goals.

Medications. Antidepressants, antipsychotic medications, anti-anxiety medications, and other medications for mental illness can

help reduce symptoms, which can help you feel less suicidal.
Addiction therapy. Treatment for drug or alcohol addiction might involve detoxification, addiction treatment programs, and self-help group sessions.
Family support and education. Your loved ones may be both a source of support and conflict. Involving them in treatment can help them understand what you're going through, give them better coping skills, and improve family communication and relationships.
Helping a loved one.
If you have a loved one who has tried suicide, or if you suspect your loved one may be at risk of doing so, obtain immediate treatment. Don't leave the individual alone.

If you have a loved one you believe may be contemplating suicide, have an open and honest talk about your worries. You may not be able to compel someone to seek professional treatment, but you may give encouragement and support. You can also help your loved one find a qualified doctor or mental health provider and make an appointment. You may even volunteer to go along.

Supporting a loved one who is chronically suicidal can be stressful and exhausting. You may be afraid and feel guilty and helpless. Take advantage of resources about suicide and suicide prevention so that you have information and tools to take action when needed. Also, take care of yourself by getting support from family, friends, organizations, and professionals.

Get active. Physical activity and exercise have been demonstrated to lessen depressive symptoms. Consider walking, running, swimming, gardening, or taking up any sort of physical exercise that you love.
Coping and help
Don't attempt to control suicidal thoughts or behavior on your own. You need expert

guidance and support to overcome the challenges associated with suicidal ideation. In addition:

Go to your appointments. Don't miss therapy sessions or doctor's visits, even if you don't want to attend or don't feel like you need to.

Take drugs as prescribed. Even if you're feeling well, don't skip your medications. If you stop, your suicidal feelings may come back. You could also experience withdrawal-like symptoms from abruptly stopping an antidepressant or other medication.

Learn about your condition. Learning about your condition can empower and motivate you to stick to your treatment plan. If you have depression, for instance, learn about its causes and treatments.

Pay attention to warning signs. Work with your doctor or therapist to identify what can trigger your suicidal emotions. Learn to detect the warning indicators early, and determine what measures to take ahead of time. Contact your doctor or therapist if you notice any changes in how you feel. Consider enlisting family members or friends in checking for warning indicators.

Make a strategy so you know what to do if suicidal thoughts resurface. You may wish to develop a written agreement with a mental health specialist or a loved one to assist you to anticipate the proper choices to do when you don't have the greatest judgment. Sharing your suicide goal with your therapist makes it feasible to foresee it and handle it.

Eliminate possible ways of harming oneself. If you fear you could act on suicide ideas, immediately get rid of any possible methods of killing yourself, such as weapons, knives, or harmful pharmaceuticals. If you take drugs that have a risk for overdose, have a family member or friend give you your pills as recommended.

Seek help from a support group. Several organizations are available to help you cope with suicidal thinking and recognize that there are many options in your life other than suicide.

Preparing for your appointment

When you call your primary care doctor to set up an appointment, you may be referred immediately to a psychiatrist. If you're in danger of killing yourself, your doctor may have you get emergency help at the hospital.

Take these steps before your appointment:

Make a list of key personal information, including any major stresses or recent life changes.

Make a list of all medications, vitamins, and other supplements that you're taking, and the doses. Be honest with your doctor about your alcohol and drug use.

Ask a family member or friend to the appointment if possible — someone who accompanies you may remember something that you missed or forgot.

Make a list of questions to ask your doctor.

Some basic questions to ask your doctor include:

Could my suicidal thoughts be linked to an underlying mental or physical health problem?

Will I need any tests for possible underlying conditions?

Do I need immediate treatment of some kind? What will that involve?

What are the alternatives to the approach that you're suggesting?

I have these other mental or physical health problems. How can I best manage them together?

Is there anything I can do to stay safe and feel better?
Should I see a psychiatrist?
Is there a generic alternative to the medicine you're prescribing me?
Are there any brochures or other printed material that I can have? What websites do you recommend?
Don't hesitate to ask additional questions.

What to expect from your doctor
Your doctor is likely to ask you many questions, such as:

When did you first begin having suicidal thoughts?
Have your suicidal thoughts been continuous or occasional?
Have you ever tried to take your own life?
Do you have the plan to kill yourself?
If you have a plan, does it involve a specific method, place, or time?
Have you made any preparations, such as gathering pills or writing suicide notes?

Do you feel like you can control your impulses when you feel like killing or hurting yourself?
Do you have friends or family members you can talk to or go to for help?
Do you drink alcohol, and if so, how much and how often?
What medications do you take?
Do you use recreational drugs?
What, if anything, helps you deal with your suicidal thoughts?
What, if anything, appears to worsen your suicidal thoughts?
What are your feelings about the future? Do you have any hope that things will improve?
Preparing and anticipating questions will help you make the most of your time with the doctor.

Take charge of your life, there is nothing you can't do, only if you believe and you're determined to do it.

Suicide is not the best route out, think about all the beautiful things you can achieve if you don't take your life.
If you feel no one loves you, I'll love to remind you that God loves you, so much that you can't understand, lean in his love, trust in him and he will direct your steps.

Shun every negative thoughts making you feel you can't do it, I was able to get up from suicidal thoughts and so you can too, everything lost can be gotten in a bigger fold but when a life is lost it's lost forever.
Love yourself and allow yourself to be loved too.

Cheers to a better life.

www.ingramcontent.com/pod-product-compliance
Lightning Source LLC
LaVergne TN
LVHW010607160826
845677LV00013B/3297

* 9 7 9 8 3 6 3 9 9 1 9 7 4 *